MAYBE HEARTS DON'T BREAK

By Courtney Nahan

ILLUSTRATIONS BY

Sakib Hassan

&

FULL PAGE ILLUSTRATIONS BY

Jessica Domnick

Instagram - @persephone.poems

DEDICATION

This book is dedicated to a young girl who didn't know she was strong and capable. To a young girl who didn't know she could handle pain or channel it. To a young girl who didn't know she would accomplish great things. To a young girl who didn't yet know that self-love is the most important kind of love.

To a young girl that used to be me.

Part 1 -

The Bending, The Bruising, The Hurting

Part 2 -

The Mending, The Stitching, The Healing

THE BENDING, THE BRUISING, THE HURTING

I've tried staying where it's safe

Far away from the deep end

Only to find out

People still drown in the shallow end

Like a car crash

At 90 miles an hour

It hits me

You're never coming back

And I need you here so badly

I'd give anything

To have you here

But you're gone

Like dust flying around my room

Lingering in my memories

Passing through my mind

But still gone

And I need you here so badly

The stars in me are dying

Burning out

Collapsing into black holes

They suck me in

They spit me out

They suck me in again

I'm lost in the universe

Floating along the Milky Way

Watching the stars shine bright

While the stars in me are dying

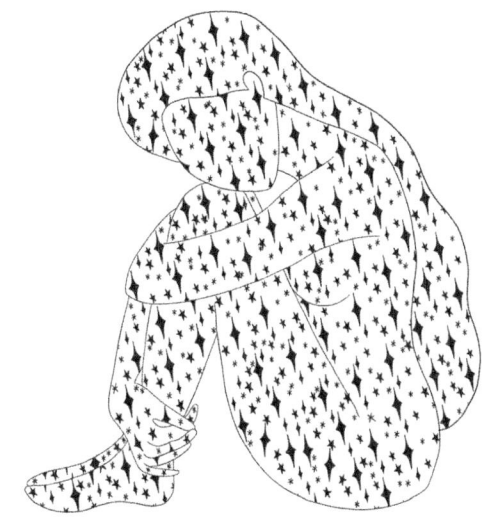

We fell together

Then fell apart

Again and again

Until we had nothing left

Dear stranger,

I saw you walking down a city street today. Your hood covered your ears so that the wind couldn't tell you its secrets. You've been running from something; I can tell by the cracks in your shoes. You've been thinking for days now; I can tell by the coldness in your eyes. I wish I could save you. To stop what you've been running from, resolve what you've been thinking of. I think of you for hours after you've passed. Maybe it's because I don't have to wonder what you're going through. Maybe because I have the same cracks in my shoes, the same coldness in my eyes. The wind has told me its secrets and I've been running next to you since.

Sincerely,

Me

I'm a cave

The farther you go

The *darker* it gets

Light struggles to shine on my deepest secrets

It took too much to hate you

It hurt too much to miss you

So I decided not to think of you

Except for the few moments

Before I rest

You come alive in these words

So I write them

And read them over again

I drown myself in the nostalgia

Then close my eyes and forget you again

Dancing through the clouds

You caught me by my wings

You cut them to pieces

Then told me to fly

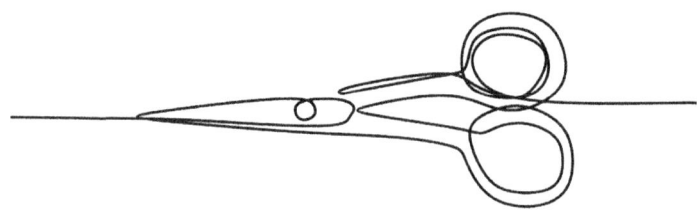

Do you remember the spring of 2010?

I woke that very first day

And I couldn't breathe

You took all the air out of my world

I should have been a flower that spring

15 years young

Brand new

Vibrant

Filled with color and innocent life

But you broke me before I could bloom

I suppose that's where it all started

The first time I felt

Betrayed

Worthless

Ugly

It's been years since that spring

And you walk around untouched

But here I am staring at the snow

Thankful I don't have to see the flowers

The ones I never got to be

Back at war with misery

Who will win?

I'm not too bad at fighting

But I'm not so sure

I won't give in

I believed with every inch of my heart that you hurting me was impossible. In my eyes you were everything good. Look at *you* now. Look at *us* now. Congratulations on making the impossible, possible.

Give me your pain

I can hold it for you

While you ride the waves

Of happiness

And I **sink** under the weight

Of the ocean

I know you're sorry
And the guilt of crushing me
Lays heavy on your mind
I know you want to mend me
Piece me back together
I know you want to heal me
To stop this pain forever
No matter how hard we try
I just can't stop ... *bleeding*

I came to you

With flowers in my hands

Roses decorated with red

You handed them back to me

And my hands were cut by the thorns

Of your rejection

There are so many words floating around in my head

I try to erase them as I lie down in bed

But regardless of how I feel in my heart

These thoughts and my head will never be apart

You changed the story

So I had to stop reading

Before the pages

Turned black

And you ruined my ending

I keep your flowers in a jar

Watching the life

Fade from bright reds

To dull browns

It reminds me

Of our dying love

Like the ashes of dead flowers

Spread amongst the spring ground

Envious of the life around them

Out of touch

But a sensory overload

I find the shadows between sunlight

And hide from the noise

If I could become one amongst the trees

So still and passed by

I'd melt into the soil and plant myself there

Only coming alive at moonlight

When the world is quiet

And the air is still

I'd give anything to disappear

Into nothingness

With the trees

Have you ever looked at your reflection

In a glass window on the side of a city street

And wondered where you went

And when you're coming back

I thought I'd come so far

Until I looked up

From the tapping of my feet

Against the cracked pavement

And realized the road had only

Just started

The outer part of me

So cold

Like armor

Impenetrable

The words you throw at me

Ricochet

And **hit** you in the heart

I bent for you

Until I *broke*

I wept for you

Until I *woke*

I cared for you

But now I *won't*

Once you've crossed a line
An ocean forms between us
With waves so big
And depths so deep
You'll never make it to me
Ever again

Overthinking

Up the mountains

And

    then

       down

          again

I watch the sunrise

And even the sound of birds

Couldn't distract me

From the thoughts in my head

The thoughts about you

And what we've been through

These empty pages have been staring back at me, begging my hand to help release these feelings. But today, this pen won't be moving. I'm out of words to write. To say I feel empty or broken would only be redundant.

I've said these words before; I've felt these feelings time after time. There hasn't been a spark of inspiration for what seems like ages. I could lie outside in the leaves staring at the stars to search for some kind of meaning, but they've lost their twinkle through my eyes and the leaves just aren't as crisp. My mind has gone thoughtless while my heart has grown sad. My eyes have gone dull while my smile has faded away. If this is how I'll be living, sometimes I think I'd rather not live at all.

I remember

You walking out the door

And the warmth you left with

It was cold in my room

Even during the summer

My skin stayed cool

Even when the sun hit it

The cold reminds me

That I'm not healed

Not even a little bit

It's funny how we used to fit

Before we tore each other apart

What was once a completed puzzle

Began to crack and gape

When we tried to put it back together

Our pieces were damaged

Ripped into different shapes

It's funny how we didn't fit anymore

How we broke each other

Tore off corners and put holes in the middle

Just to make us into different pieces

To fit a different puzzle

I hope life treats you differently
Than it has treated *me*

"Gone"

She wakes in the early morning as the sun begins to leave its streaks of light across her white sheets. Birds are chirping and the air is still. It is almost perfect.

But she also wakes to an empty spot next to her in bed. She reaches out to feel the bed is firm, like no one had slept there the night before. Because no one had. For the first time in years, she slept alone. He wasn't on a trip; he wasn't at work. He was gone. Like his things from the closet, like the pictures around the room, like the air they shared together, like the memories they could have made. Just gone.

She reaches under her pillow to find a phone with no messages left for her. So she begins to type one herself.

"I miss you" She types. She deletes it.

"I love you" She types. She deletes it.

She lies there until better words come to find her.

"I still remember slow dancing in our friend's kitchen together while everyone else forgot we were there. The first time I really looked into your eyes. The lights were dim but I saw you perfectly. We were laughing so hard you almost dropped me on the floor. I never told you that was my favorite memory, I never got to tell you that was my favorite way you've ever looked at me. I didn't get to tell you these things before you turned your back and left"

She lies back down and lets the emptiness consume her back to sleep.

There are wounds that won't heal

They just keep seeping

Staining the floor red

Leaving a trail of pain

For one to retrace *over and over*

As if open skin doesn't burn enough

The weakness that comes with losing so much

Leaves you wishing you'd bleed out

And find **blackness** in the sea of red

I loved you
I loved you and you turned away
I would have given you anything
I would have even begged you to stay
I was willing to give you everything
Take pieces of me and glue them to you
I was willing to be anything
Love you until my face turned blue
I loved you and you left me
In the middle of the road
Where the cars passed me
And not one of them slowed
I loved you and you shot me
Directly in the heart
I loved you
Even if we finished before we got to start

The real damage isn't something you can *touch*

It's not something you can *see*

The real damage is in the way I *walk*

It's in the way I *speak*

Shades of black

Intertwined in my being

I try to see color

But darkness is all I'm seeing

I'm crumbling

Saying things I don't mean

Making promises I can't keep

Forgive me

It's just a phase

I'll be better

When I'm back together

The moon used to save me

When the sun ducked behind the mountains

The moon's light would guide my way

But it seems the moon is hiding from me

She's tucked behind the clouds

Shying away from my pain

Maybe she can't take it anymore

Carrying my load

Maybe her heart has grown cold

In the process of mending mine

I miss her

My moon

Because without her light

My heart bleeds at night

I try my best

To mean what I say

But it seems to be

That my words are

Too big
For my voice to hold

Death is

Crossing a bridge to nowhere

Watching your heart flee into the sky

Death is

Missing a piece of your body

Letting the nightmares steal it away

Death is

Misery and its company

Wearing sadness like an old coat

Death is

Unimaginable

Like the depths of the universe

Stretching on forever with no end

Death is

Aching

Waiting to wake up and see you again

The memory

It comes in waves

Building

       Building

              Building

Until it crashes upon me

It overwhelms me

Takes the air from my lungs

Speeds my heart rate

Nearly takes me from this world

It leaves me paralyzed on the floor

I'm left with my palms turned up

Begging to never remember again

But I remember

The memory

Every single day

Dear old flame,

I don't know how to tell you how much I loved you. It burned inside of me like a fire. Every time I looked at you my heart sparked a flame. Now when I see you, smoke fills my lungs from the burnt out match. I look at you and remember how it felt to be so close to you, to feel your soul in mine. Now all I feel is the lingering thought that we should some-how, someway still be one.

Sincerely,

Me

Not yet pouring the pills

Down the drain

I'm saving them

For a day that rains

It felt wrong

All of it

The scene

The lighting

The sounds

I went for it anyway

But there ended up being

A price to pay

If you take my hand
I will eventually let it go
For I don't stay too long
In places where **love grows**

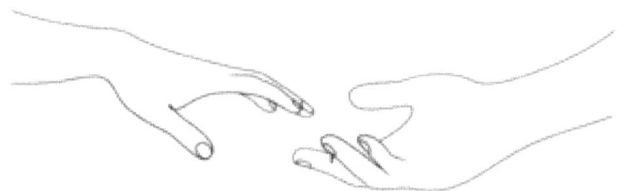

You've gone away

Far enough that I can't chase you

You haven't even left footprints in the sand

So that I could follow you

What could I have done

To make leaving me *so easy*?

Standing alone

On the edge

Wondering

If anyone could ache as much *as I do*

It was a better time

When fairytales

And magic

Were all we knew

> Now we know
>
> That our fairytales
>
> Don't have happy endings
>
> And magic isn't real

My worst fears

Come true in the dark

I roll over to find an empty spot

And a cold pillow

Only to wish

You were here

To give me sweet dreams

Once again

Standing still

So peaceful

Then it lights on fire

And crumbles to the ground

Please come home

Rebuild this paper house

Stay with me

Hang our paintings on the wall

And put our pictures on the mantle

Please come home

Help me stand still

And be so peaceful

Rebuild this paper house

If I knew then

What I know now

I would have never

Let your fingertips

Touch my naked skin

I would have swallowed

The *feeling*

I wouldn't have let you

Sink in

So far down

That my bones

Began to need you

And my heart

Began to beg for you

If I knew then

What I know now

I would have never

Let you *love* me

Letting go of you felt like a storm

Like the moon backed away

And the tides rushed the shores

Sweeping away a piece of my being

You can't tell me I haven't lived
When I'd rather make mistakes
Than to get it right

I wrote this book

Then set it on fire

I started from the beginning

And called myself a liar

It's hard to read my work

When I separate myself in two

I wonder why I do that

Maybe it's because of you

I was damaged in your eyes

You were damaged in mine

Funny how we found each other

As all damaged people do

There is no medication
For heartache

Sometimes I sit and think about all of the things
I've lost and I ask the universe

                           why it takes good things
from me

Watching all the promises you made

Blow away with the wind

> *Falling*

Into the ocean

Drowning in the abyss

It's been years

Or maybe just months

      Any time without you

      Feels like forever

When I finally stop aching

It'll be because I have nothing left

Nothing to give

Nothing to say

Nothing to think

I'll be nothing

When I finally stop aching

I became everything you needed

When you were tired

I was caffeine

When you were thirsty

I was water

When you were broken

I was your bandaid

When you were all better

I was abandoned

And as you left

My heart cried out

Then suddenly

I was thankful

That the cries of the heart

Can only be felt and not heard

He wiped away
All of the kisses
That landed on her skin
Falling from the moonlight
He washed his hands in the river
And left her bare
Out in the open
For all of the stars to see
She touched her skin
Where the moon had kissed her
And missed the way it felt
Before he came along
And washed away
All the good things
She had ever held

I remember the first time my heart *cracked*

And all the times after that

I remember the way it felt

The way that I fell

I remember you standing over me

Watching me suffer

I reached for your hand

And I watched you walk away

Like bitter medication on a spoon

I swallowed my pride

And bent at your feet

I kissed the ground

And said thank you

For stealing everything

I ever called my own

For taking away all the things

I ever loved

I said thank you

Because you told me to

I swallowed my pride

Because you told me to

I would have done

Anything for you

I was blinded

I was chained

I did it all because you told me to

Watch the sky

When the clouds turn gray

Know that my soul is flying

Under the darkness

And into the storm

Like star-crossed lovers

We danced through the night

Little did I know

You'd break my heart by daylight

I craved what I couldn't have

A sense of myself

Succumbed to your flesh

I craved what you couldn't give

My soul

Smashed into glass shards

I craved what we couldn't do

Love

A beating heart

Dying in what used to be

Standing next to you

Under a starlit sky

Something was wrong

I told myself not to worry

Monsters don't live in you

But I was once blinded too

You bring me out

Of my deepest

Darkest depths

Unlock my inner demon

Cracking out of its shell

I want you to touch me

In places I've never been touched

I want to taste you

On the skin around my lips

I want all of the bad things

That would make my angels blush

You bring me out

Of my deepest

Darkest depths

It can feel like nothing
    Like the invisibility of air
        Surrounding everything
            But being nothing at all

Your lips looked r*ed*
They tasted *blue*
All of your words
Were never *true*

I dreamed a dream

Where I lost it all

I woke up and realized

It wasn't a dream *at all*

"Let it go"

She remembers walking around that beach house, hearing the waves crash against the dock. The air was always warm and the skies were always blue. What a magical feeling to be in the most perfect place at the most perfect time.

But now that house is empty, the people are gone, only memories are left on the wall. Instead of the warm air and blue skies, this day her thoughts brought gray clouds and a chill in the breeze. Her room smelled of salty tears and heartache.

There is no loss like death. There is no loss like death because there is no hope. There is no hoping she's going to catch him walking down the street, there is no hoping he's going to burst into her room with laughter, there is no hoping that she'll feel his embrace again, see his face again, hear his voice again. Death is hopeless.

As if he heard her thoughts from a lifetime away, she heard his voice in her head.

"Let it go" He said. As he always said.

So she wiped her eyes and did as he said. She let

him go. Except this time she hoped she'd see him when she gets to wherever he is.

Your words turn to dust

As soon as they hit the air

They used to be butterflies

Floating into my ears

Perching themselves so quietly

Now everything you say to me

Falls flat

Flat like the way my heart deflates

When you break another promise

I opened up to you

Like a butterfly in the spring

But you rained on me

And broke my wings

I thought my worst fear was losing you

I thought the impact would knock me backwards

But instead the impact was still

Barely noticeable

It's the part that comes next

That has become my worst fear

The missing

The longing

The waking up each day without you

The memories

The love

All of it dispersing into thin air

It would be

less painful

Carving your name into my skin

Than it would be to love you again

It was easy to break down these walls

Once I realized it would **never** be a castle

It was easy to cross that bridge

Once I realized you'd **never** be my prince

When I roll over

I can only hope it'll all be over

I'm intoxicated

And these empty bottles on the shelf

Are revealing all of my secrets

The scary kind

The kind that comes up

And you push it right back down

Chasing it

Drowning it

Until the bottles are empty

Like broken clocks
    We lost our time
        You moved on
            But left me behind

And there I went

Falling

     Falling

          Falling

Until the only thing

Left beneath me

Was the end of the world

Dear ex-lover,

It started out with hope, didn't it? Two young kids on a path over the rainbow. It didn't take us long before we figured out there was no gold on the other side. Instead we found ruins. Pieces of our hearts splayed across the ground, intertwining with the crumbling leaves. We tried to pick them up, we did. But the pieces were so small they slipped through the cracks of our fingers. We had nothing left, so we clawed at everything and nothing at all. Isn't that what forever is? A bunch of timeless nothings? Or was the nothingness always going to be reserved for just us?

Signed,

Me

You smiled

And my world

Didn't stop spinning

And that's when I knew

You weren't for *me*

And I wasn't for *you*

I see right through
Your false intentions
I know better now

Maybe bruised hearts love more

Because I've never loved you more

Than when you walked out the door

The best advice I can give is because of the worst mistakes I have made.

What a peaceful morning

Blue birds are singing outside

The coffee is hot in its cup

But her mind is scattered

And her heart is longing for something

That it cannot reach

Why is her uncertainty

Clashing with the peace that surrounds her?

THE MENDING, THE STITCHING, THE HEALING

It is your new job

To *never* forget

The way you've been hurt

The way you've been burned

The way you've been crushed

Because it all comes back around

And you owe it to yourself

To not have to learn the lesson *twice*

You will be cut

And sewn back together

Many times

Fearless:

Is someone who has broken the generational curse, someone who riots against their past and wins the war.

Like the flowers growing out of my mind

I am blossoming into a better me

Someone who is gracious and kind

Forgiving and understanding

I am no longer afraid to be delicate

To be fragile

Like the petals on a white rose

I am no longer afraid to be sharp

To be strong willed

Like the thorns popping from its stem

I am blossoming

Into a beautiful bouquet of flowers

And you'll find all the colors of me there

All I ask in return is that you treat me with care

I'm not the girl that I once was. And the girl I once was, wasn't the girl I was before that. Time changes everyone, *time and time again.*

I want to be the stars in your sky

The ones you look up to

When the tears roll down your cheeks

I want to be your solace on the darkest nights

The stars that shine in your eyes

And line your soul

I've got a piece of your heart
That beats next to mine
On the sleepless
Lonely nights

I gasped

As he fingered

Through my thoughts

And looked past my words

Leaving me waiting for solace

Or the resolution

That always comes next

Dear lesson,

I've made a lot of mistakes but you weren't one of them. I can still feel the way our arms locked around each other, trust growing in our chests. I can remember the hand holds, swinging our arms back and forth between our beating hearts. I can still feel the way your eyes felt when they looked me over like I came from the sky. But I can also remember the crumbling of my palace the day you walked away. The way the bricks fell and broke against the ground. The way my hand caught on fire and burned when you pulled yours away, the way your eyes looked when they went as cold as that December night. Through the loving and the aching came lessons that were learned in between the fine lines. I'm better now, I'm stronger now.

I now know love and I now know pain.

Thank you,

Me

And I'd choose *you*

Through winds

That could blow **love** away

Finding that perfect rhythm

Between two heartbeats

Is like finally finding gold

At the end of that rainbow

On a sunny day

After the storm has passed

And the world has settled

Two heartbeats

Beating as one

You are worth
What you're afraid to take

As his kisses

Planted

    down

      my

        skin

I told myself

To let him in

That the past

Is behind me

And to allow the lips

Of new-found hope

To bring me peace

We made it when we thought we wouldn't

When the moon pulled the tides

That flooded the land

We somehow

Made it to higher ground

She's like

Listening to your favorite song

In the middle of June

With your windows down

Letting the wind

Sweep away all of your doubts

I'd walk on water

And search its depths

For a trace of your love

Your eyes are like photographs

Of a time I've seen before

They tell the same old story

Of love

Loss

And more

So take my hand

Look back into my eyes

And tell me secrets

Of a time I haven't yet seen

Of a place I've never been

Today I caught a glimpse of the old me.

I felt amazing.

I was everything I used to be: I was talkative, I laughed at everything, got along with everyone, smiled and meant it.

I was happy for that moment in time.

I was me.

I hope she stays.

The old me would have screamed
The new me spoke
With dignity and confidence
She is matured
She is ready
For all the that life throws at her
All because the old me
Learned her lessons

I still remember the first time I saw you
Your aura radiated nostalgia
Of a time where I wanted something
So much more than I wanted air

Love me in the morning

After the tea has brewed

Kiss me on my forehead

Admire all my hues

Sing your passion to me

Reach out for my hand

And tell me what you see

Give me all the love you have

Tell me that you're enamored

Erase all of my bad

Tell me that you love me

And I'll say **I love you** too

Remember who you are

Even when it gets dark

Remember to be your own *light*

When all is still

Listen to your heart

She's whispering secrets

And telling the truth

Listen to her

And you shall be free

I will be more than I was yesterday

Even if that means I can't take you with me

You forgot to water me

So I dried up

And fell apart

Next time I grow

I'll remember to water myself

"Today she found a letter"

It was a new place, a new time. The leaves were made of bright oranges and deep browns as they crunched beneath the shoes of everyone walking by her window. The crisp air, the early sunsets, all of it felt like starting over, a chance to become something she wasn't before. But it was scary as all new things are.

"You know" Her roommate says "You *can* unpack your things." She smiles as she heads for the door. She smiles back and looks at her luggage around the room. Untouched. She reaches for the small shoebox next to her bed and decides to open that one first.

Inside are pictures of her past. Happy times, sad times and everything in between. She flicks between the pictures, the folded up pieces of poetry, the concert tickets, a few second place ribbons and torn up paper. But at the very bottom she finds a note. One she forgot ever existed. It was from him.

It was dated December 5, 2009.

He wrote: "You're beautiful and much more capable than you think. I see behind your walls. There's a strong, resilient girl in there. Let her breathe."

Her breath catches as she folds the note and puts it back at the bottom of the shoe box.

As she shuts the lid she thinks: After all these years who knew his words would be the ones she needed to hear most.

And when she stopped letting him steal her light

She shined brighter than every star in the night sky

A smile made of promises
And a heart made of broken chains
She was a beautiful
Contradiction

Extending myself to reach you

I'm aching for your touch

Wrap me up in roses

Offer my soul for you to crush

I'll give you every piece of me

Sing your words into my soul

I'll strip my skin for you to see

All the things I've ever been

And all the things that we could be

Even the stars in space

Cry sometimes

I feel them on my skin

When they fall on my face

They remind me

That the tears in my eyes

Even the drops so small

Are worth more than the sky

Since the moment I saw you

I was drawn to your movement

The way you pushed your hair back

From out of your eyes

The way you looked at the ground

When you contemplated

Your next words

The way your hands moved

When they interlaced with mine

And I have to admit

I haven't been able to look away since

She is a wild rose

Covered in thorns

I heard if you hurt her

You'll always be scorned

If you love me

Like I love your smile

I promise

I'll be worth your while

Princess of the stars

Queen of the night

You keep the planets aligned

You bring us all light

I can close my eyes

And instantly go back

I can feel every feeling

I can remember every moment

I can take this pen

And write like it happened yesterday

Because that's what you've done to me

Whatever you did

It lasts

It lingers

It climbs to the very top of my heart

And jumps to the pit of my stomach

I don't have to worry much

About holding on for dear life

Because I can close my eyes

I don't have to fight

To feel your love

Like it was just yesterday

Do not paint yourself

Into a pretty picture

That is not yours

Color yourself

In hues of your own

And paint a picture

That belongs to you

Speak kind words to me

Heal me

From the inside out

Tell me that I shine

Tell me that you're mine

Tell me I'm the prettiest thought

That's ever crossed your mind

Maybe everyone thought I was beautiful

Maybe it was my own reflection telling me I wasn't

Maybe I was happy

Maybe it was my past inflicting the pain

Maybe I was good enough

Maybe it was my insecurities telling me I wasn't

Maybe everything was okay

Maybe I convinced myself I wasn't

Awake covered in white sheets

I feel you underneath of me

The sun peaks through

My broken blinds

A streak of sunlight

Brightens your eyes

I look deep

Deep enough to find your soul

I kiss your lips

This is heaven

Heaven on earth

Dear love,

The unknown secrets of the ocean couldn't reach deep enough to express my love. I've waited lifetimes to feel what I feel in my chest. You move me over mountains and swim with me overseas. You make me feel like the wind could take me flying with the way it carries our secrets. I want to bury myself in your chest, just as far as I can go. I want you to tuck me in as the storm swirls around us. The sun itself couldn't compare to your light, the moon could never compare to the pull of your tides. I want you to know that you are half of me. You make up my very nature. I want you to know that I love you and I've just tried my best to put it into words.

Love,

Me

Forgiving myself

Has been the toughest obstacle

This far

But I'm determined to do it

If you cannot stay with me

I'll write you in this book

And have these words forever

I'll trace them over when I'm bruised and sore

If anything else

That's what love is for

Your body

Is not a vessel for pain

Nor is pain

A fictional thing

Let your pain live

In a place outside of you

Let it create beautiful things

Think of each of my mistakes

As a coat in the summer time

They layer and layer

Suffocating me

Think of my lessons

As stripping those coats

And letting my skin absorb

The summer sun

We can't all have sunshine

The earth needs its rain

But as much as it needs the rain

We make our rotation

To find the sun *once again*

"You fixed me"

They sit on the couch talking and reminiscing about their first date.

That night she wore a green shirt with her hair pulled back away from her face. He wore a black shirt and beat up old jeans. The moment their eyes met, magic became real. What a shimmery, enchanting night they both agreed.

But as she sits there and watches him smile, she can't help but go back to a time where her heart ached more than it smiled. She thought about those lonely nights, the longing, the crying, the hurting. She remembers her reflection in the mirror, tired eyes and messy hair. She remembers the worried looks on the people around her. She remembers the marks on her wrists from squeezing too tight when the world seemed to crush her. She remembers the note she wrote when she didn't think she could make it. She remembers it all, all of the time before she met him.

She looks at him still smiling on the couch and says,

"You know you fixed me"

He laughed and questioned her.

"You brought light into my life when there was only darkness. You sang love into my ears when all I could hear were the thoughts in my head. You breathed life into my lungs when all I could smell was the smoke from my burnt out flame. You loved me when I was afraid to love myself. You showed me I was deserving, that I was worthy, that I was beautiful." She pauses.

"You fixed me."

I found peace
        In my loneliness
            I found solace
                In the quiet
                    I found love
                        In my reflection

You lie me down

On red velvet cushions

So they won't show

The pain pouring from my body

You take your time

Kissing all of my open wounds

They heal with your **love**

They close

And turn into scars

She's a quiet mountain

Looming in the night

You wonder

What made her grow

Tall enough to see over the trees

You wonder

What makes her so quiet

Against the wind that howls

You wonder

Why she is so solemn

Under a sky full of stars

Here we are

Dancing between

These flashing lights

Your kiss hits me

And we spin in the dark

You look at me

And I feel like the only girl in the world

I tell you love feels like this

And for the first time

I mean it

It was cold that winter night

My breath made circles in the frigid air

We ran out into the middle of the street

And caught snowflakes on our tongues

And swam around in the sea of white

I remember it so fondly

That time we were kids

I'd go back over and over

If only I could

I love you in a way

    I've never been able to love

        Or be loved

You have all of my pieces

One by one they jumped into you

Aligning themselves

Alongside of you

Following you to the end

I can't forget those eyes
And the way they saw my soul
I'd love to see you again
Even if it's just in my dreams

I hope you love

Like the forest on fire

Passionate and fierce

I hope you cry

Like the waterfalls

Falling to their destiny

I hope you live

Like the sun

Gone and back again

But always there

Dear young woman,

I saw you there, standing in the middle of spring. The grass was green and freshly cut beneath your feet. The sun was shining down on your skin, making it warm to the touch. The air smelled of flowers and hope. I wished this for you. I dreamt this for you. To feel a sense of freedom. To be broken out of the chains of the winter's cold heart. I hope you stay here, in the middle of spring. I'll wish it for you. I'll dream it for you.

Sincerely,

Me

It's September and your stars are in my sky
The air is warm and it still has your smell
I think about the last time we were here
And I remember it all like I remember you
It's September and your hand is in mine
The night is cool and it kisses me where you did
I think about that crooked smile on your lips
And I remember it all like I know I shouldn't
It's September and your words are in my ear
My bed is empty but your warmth is still here
I think about the memories between these sheets
And I remember it all like I remember September

I talk to her

Like she's a friend

The ghost of me

From a past life

We mend each other

Here and there

Wound by wound

Stitch by stitch

I wear her like

A second skin

I warm her when she's cold

I'm her comfort when she's scared

The ghost of me

She'll always be there

I want you to love me for me

So that all of my flaws

Stitch together

And make me **whole**

Being yourself
Is not one version
Being yourself
    Means bending
    Means breaking
    It means growing
    And changing
Call it a process
Being yourself is
A work in progress

The melody of your voice

Sways me

Into a universe

Made for loving you

With luck on my side

I'll be able to keep you here

With me

For the rest of our forever

Nothing can compare

To the songs

I hear our stories in

Reminding me of happiness

And a time where it all mattered

"What would it be like to fall"

The trees look different from up here. Seeing the tops of them was like being close to the sky. Like you could jump on top of them and reach heaven.

She sits on the edge of the cliff she hiked miles to get to. Close enough to feel the exhilaration of being so far away from solid ground but far enough away that she couldn't fall. The world in front of her is so peaceful. But something within her is stirring, like the wind that blows through her hair.

She moves closer to the edge and thinks about what it would feel like to fall. Would it feel like escaping? Would it feel like regret? She ponders these thoughts over and over again. Until she hears something behind her.

Before she can look back, he is sitting next to her. Silent. Not saying a word. The quiet isn't uncomfortable though; it is the solace her stirring heart has wished for.

After a while their sweet silence breaks when he says: "Do you ever wonder what it would be like to fall?"

Peace surrounds them knowing they're not alone.

Point me in the direction of heaven

I have someone I'd like to talk to

You traced over me

Like I was made of paper

And your hand a pen

You wrote your favorite songs

And drew me tiny pictures

But it was the love between the lines

That made my heart fly

You dressed me

In diamonds

Filled with your love

I've loved my reflection

Every day since

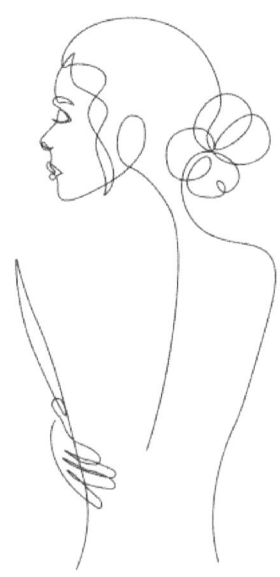

You gave me so much more
Than I could ever get back
So I took and I took
Until I was full
Then I realized
Having everything is nothing
When you have nothing to give

I could tell you about it

Until my breath is gone

I love you

And I know our hearts belong

Looking into your eyes

I see the way we'll dance

The way we'll sing along to the radio

I see the way you'll hold my hand

The way you'll hold me in bed

I see us cooking breakfast

The way we'll eat it in the morning sun

I see our future together

The way we'll always be as one

If there is any hope left

Hand it to me

I'll put it in a glass jar

And I'll protect it with my life

And as the wars around me
Started to increase
It was within myself
That I finally found peace

My heart didn't know where it was going
My feet merely followed
I traveled for miles
Walked through deserts
Swam through oceans
Took flight in the sky
When I finally stopped and looked down
My feet were pointed towards you

Your open cuts
They will become scars
And your scars
They will become reminders
And your reminders
They will become reason
And your reason
It will become strength
And your strength
It will become love

Let's not talk about how *hard* it was
Let's focus on how you made it *livable*

Dear old self,

I'm writing this to you, maybe you'll see this. Maybe you won't. But it's worth a try. I'm proud of you. Such a tough little girl. You've made it through things you never thought you could. You put your walls up nice and high and kept yourself safe.

Lately people have been asking for you. They're asking where you went.

What they don't know is that you have blossomed. You are a different "you" now. We are a different "me" now.

I'm sorry I left you behind. Hidden behind those walls. I moved on and I almost forgot what you felt like. The pain you endured, the battles you fought alone. I'm sorry I didn't take the time to heal you. So here I am asking for your forgiveness. Asking you to see what we've become. I'm asking you to walk along next to me. Oh, the team we could be.

Read this over and hopefully give this life another chance

- *The me without you*

Maybe hearts don't break

Maybe they just bend

    And bruise

      Stretch

        And crack

Maybe they only hurt

So we can never truly lose it all

Maybe hearts don't break

So we can always get back up when we fall

- Courtney

Printed in Great Britain
by Amazon